Squeeze the Pennies to Make the Nickels Count:

Frugal Living Tips and Tricks

By: Tracey Glenn

Copyright 2017, Tracey Glenn

Frugal living, what is the meaning of this? Living below your means, spending less than you earn. It doesn't mean you are a cheapskate or poor, it means you are being smart about how you are spending your money, reaching important goals, paying off debt, or building a comfortable retirement for yourself and family. With the ever-rising cost of living these days, many of us are left just trying to make ends meet. Not much is getting cheaper.

Sometimes it's hard to go without certain things when it seems like everyone else around you have everything — but that doesn't mean it's real or they're not in debt up to their designer sunglasses. Even the rich people get in over their heads trying to keep up with the Joneses that they envy. The cost of "trying to have it all" is often a lifetime of debt, stress and, of course, *working to pay for it all.* So, if you are struggling just to pay your bills each month, are in debt, or just want to save money, then living below your means by incorporating a frugal lifestyle might be just the answer you are looking for.

Below, in no particular order, is a compiled list of frugal tips and tricks that I have found to be helpful in stretching our money, mostly out of necessity and partially to see how much we could save. Some of these tips might seem obvious to you if you're already a "penny pincher," but I know that my family often spends extra money unnecessarily. Are you ready to squeeze those pennies to make the nickels count? Ok…Let's go!

- Use a foam soap dispenser, fill ¼ of bottle with hand soap and the rest with water, shake to mix.

- Create a budget that works for your family. Figure out where all of your money is going and be realistic about your spending.

- Track your spending. There are apps that can do it for you or just use an old checking account register.

- Live within your means. Better than that, try to live below your means.

- Avoid shopping just because you are bored and need something to do. Visit your closet and create new outfits.

- If you do shop online, try looking on Google for promo codes for discounts and free shipping.

- Stop online shopping impulsively. Shop only when you really need an item.

- Visit yard/garage sales for great deals. You might find that toy your child wants for $2.00 verses $20.00 at the store.

- Don't throw something away without trying to make money off of it. Broken items can be sold as parts.

- Don't live on credit and use credit cards irresponsibly.

- Use the points or cash back on your credit cards if your card offers them.

- Use the teller machine networked for your bank to avoid transaction fees.

- Check out thrift stores or consignment shops before stopping by the department stores if you need new clothes.

- Shop consignment or thrift stores on sale days, if they have them.

- If you must go to a retail store, look in the sale/clearance section before looking at the full priced areas.

- Save money by buying items when they are out of season. This is an awesome way to get more bang for your buck.

- Avoid the mall. You'll be amazed at how much money you will save simply by staying out of the mall if you are a frequent shopper.

- Adopt a simpler wardrobe. Buy clothing that can be interchanged.

- Don't buy Dry-Clean only clothes. If you do need Dry-Clean only clothing, use an at home dry-cleaning solution.

- Exchange baby/children's clothes with friends or neighbors. Clothing swaps can be a great way to save money and recycle gently used clothes.

- Shop for free, look on Craigslist, Freecycle, IWANNA, Facebook, Curbside.

- Avoid buying the latest technology. Wait a while and the price will be significantly lower.

- Combine your trips around town to be most fuel efficient.

- Don't speed. Speeding tickets are expensive and can raise your insurance rates.

- Ask for your child's good grades discount on your automobile insurance if applicable.

- Take a driver's education course for a discount.

- Ask your insurance company if discounts are available and what they are.

- Pay for your insurance annually. Most insurance companies charge an extra $5.00 to break up the bill into payments.

- Research different routes to work to save time and gas.

- Wear your clothes more than once to save on wear and tear and laundry cost.

- Cut back on baths and showers. Do you really need to take 2-3 a day?

- Only wash your hair every other day.

- Brush and floss daily. Good mouth hygiene can prevent problems later.

- Use less toothpaste. Do you really need to apply toothpaste from the front of the brush to the back? A drop will be enough.

- Don't overspend on hygiene products. Use coupons or sign up for free products.

- At the end of the toothpaste tube? Cut the end and squeeze out the rest.

- Use a reusable water bottle. This will keep those plastic bottles out of the land field.

- Coupon, but don't buy products you won't use. That's money wasted not money saved.

- Skip the convenience stores. The prices are generally higher.

- Use weather strip around doors and windows. Be sure to keep doors and windows closed when cold or hot.

- Air seal your home, add insulation if needed.

- Contact your local electric company or organization to get a free energy saving kit.

- Contact your local fire station if you don't have a smoke detector. Change the batteries every few months.

- Invest in CFL or LED bulbs.

- Invest in a surge protector to protect your investments.

- Invest in low flow toilets and showerheads.

- Take shorter showers. So much money is wasted here.

- Turn off the water when you're not using it, such as brushing your teeth, washing your hair, shaving.

- Use your towel more than once to save on laundry. Hang to dry and reuse.

- Don't invest in expensive razors, you can maintain a cheap razor by wiping it clean and adding a light coat of petroleum jelly every now and then to prevent rust.

- Only run washing machines and dishwashers when full.

- Follow the laundry detergent directions and use only what is needed. Better yet, make your own!

- Use cold water in the washing machine.

- Line dry clothing if possible.

- Skip the heat dry cycle on the dishwasher and air dry.

- Instead of using a dishwasher, hand wash dishes and air dry.

- Replace your paper towels and paper napkins with cloth napkins and hand towels.

- Go over your cell phone bill and cancel services you don't use. Why pay for 20 GB of data if you only use 1GB.

- Consider a pre-paid cell phone if you don't use a lot of data and minutes.

- When purchasing cell phones, avoid cell phone payment plans if you can. Buying cellphone outright saves money in the long run.

- Cancel the cable or satellite channels you are not using. Why pay for those 115 channels you never watch?

- Cancel cable altogether and go with Netflix or Hulu. There are thousands of movies and season shows available.

- Cancel your land line phone. If don't use it you really won't miss it.

- Do not pay for beauty treatments, make your own bath bombs and facial scrubs.

- Get a jar of extra virgin coconut oil. Not only is it great for cooking, It's great for skin and hair care.

- Consider doing your own hair and nails instead of going to a pricey salon.

- Invest in certain items that can save you money long term: a crock pot, pressure cooker, food dehydrator, canning supplies, bread machine, deep chest freezer, green bags for produce etc.

- Reuse plastic groceries bags as trash bags.

- Purchase reusable grocery bags, some stores charge for the plastic grocery bags.

- Purchase reusable plastic containers instead of plastic sandwich and storage bags.

- Sell your recycling products. Earn money for soda cans, plastic bottles, etc.

- Unplug devices when not in use to save power. A lot of devices use "ghost power" when they are plugged up even when they are not being used.

- Utilize online bill pay through your bank. This can help avoid late fees.

- Keep up with your bills due by date to avoid late fees. Who wants to pay an extra $5.00 on their bills?

- Before buying a big ticket-item wait at least 30 days to think about it. This can also give you time to see if the item goes on sale.

- Compare car insurance companies to find a cheaper rate. It never hurts to shop around.

- Use the free envelopes sent in your bills, add a stamp and cover their label with your own.

- Budget in holidays, anniversaries, birthdays, graduations. It's better to be prepared than to spend extra money when they come up.

- Plan for gifts and buy when items are on sale or on clearance. It's better to have items on hand and avoid last minute shopping.

- Check out the library for books, CDs, and DVDs instead of buying them. You can enjoy them and then return without adding clutter to your home.

- If you are wanting to purchase books, CDs, and DVDs, try to buy them pre-owned. Most of the time you can buy them in like new condition for a lot cheaper than full retail price.

- Attend wellness clinics to take advantage of free or low-cost test and services.

- Get your annual check-ups. If there's any problems it's better to find them and get treated earlier than later.

- Consider getting a flu shot if you are able.

- Make sure your families shots are up to date.

- Use walk-in clinics instead of an emergency room for non-emergency medical care.

- Keep your hands clean. This will help cut back on germs being passed around.

- Ask for your doctor for generic medicine if you need a prescription. Also ask for samples.

- Consider 3 month supplies of prescription medicine thru mail order if your insurance plan allows this.

- Look for discount cards for medicine online. Most discount cards won't double with insurance cards.

- Take medication as directed. Don't skip doses to save money.

- Join the reward programs for the stores you shop at frequently. You can earn "points" just for shopping and get discounts later.

- Use social media for discounts. "Like" certain brands on Facebook to get coupons.

- Skip the car wash and do it yourself. Great exercise and saves money too.

- Consider doing your own yardwork if your able. Hire the teenager in the family or neighborhood instead of a lawncare service if you're not able to do it yourself.

- Clean your own home if you are able.

- Make your coffee at home, avoid the pricey coffee bars. Buy a quality coffee maker and brew as much as you want.

- Bake your own family's birthday cakes and have parties at home.

- Invest in reusable coffee pods instead of buying the expensive ones and fill with your favorite coffee.

- Invest in reusable coffee filters instead of one use paper filters.

- Take your lunch to work. What better way to use those leftovers.

- Eat out less often. Save the restaurants for a special occasion. Use a coupon or go before the dinner time to save even more.

- A lot of restaurants offer free food if it's your birthday. You might get embarrassed by the staff singing Happy Birthday to you but you get free food.

- Use your leftovers or freeze them for later meals. Leftover vegetables are great for soups and broths.

- Have a meatless meal. Beans and rice can fill you up as much as steak and potatoes can.

- Desserts and sweets in moderation. Lots of calories and no nutrition. Cut back to save calories and money.

- Alcohol in moderation. Even one beer a day can add up to a lot of money each month.

- Quit smoking. If you're not able to quit cut back on the amount you smoke.

- Cut out expensive gym memberships. There are plenty of YouTube videos or Pinterest ideas.

- Cancel memberships and subscriptions you are not using.

- Sell your clutter or unused items. You can earn money and declutter at the same time.

- Go with one car if you are able. You will save money not having to maintain multiple vehicles.

- Go with a smaller fuel-efficient vehicle if you are able.

- Make sure your tires are properly inflated.

- Go with a smaller home. A smaller home can mean a lower power bill, cheaper taxes, etc.

- Drink more water and less soda.

- Find a bank with a free checking or savings account. Why pay them to be their customer.

- Turn down the thermostat in the winter. It's cheaper to put on a sweater or snuggle in a blanket.

- Turn up the thermostat in the summer. It's cheaper to wear shorts than to keep your home at 65 degrees.

- Run fans to stay cool.

- Turn down the hot water heater to 120. Most are set at 140.

- Change/clean air conditioner filters regularly.

- Close blinds in the summer to keep your home cooler.

- Open blinds in the winter so the sunshine can help heat your home.

- Make your own "green" cleaners. Baking soda, vinegar, lemon juice, peroxide, alcohol, are just a few items you can clean with.

- Borrow items that you may only need once or every now and then.

- Have a no-spend weekend, week, or month.

- When traveling, pack your own lunch, snacks and drinks.

- Consider a local vacation or a staycation.

- Check out your local area for festivals, concerts, museums, special events, lakes, and parks.

- Invite friends over instead of going out. Bring out the board games and have some old fashion fun.

- When entertaining make it a potluck event. Everyone brings a dish to share.

- Meal plan and grocery shop with a list. Set a budget and stick to it.

- Don't buy any kind of diet "stuff".

- Buy fruits and vegetable that are in season.

- Check out weekly ads before shopping. Plan meals around the sales.

- Avoid grocery shopping on an empty stomach. When you shop hungry you are tempted to purchase items not on your list

- Plan in for one or two extra items that are marked down so much you can't pass up the deal.

- Consider store brands vs name brand. Usually, but not always, store brands are just as good as name brand.

- Try to shop alone to avoid buying unplanned items. How many times have you been shopping with the family and ended up with Disney Cars fruit snacks and extra cereal because Elsa was on the cover.

- Compare the price per ounce cost of each item. Sometimes the larger containers are not always the better price.

- When checking out at stores always watch for price mistakes and make sure if you use coupons they are taken off.

- Go shopping earlier in the day, look for marked down items. You can save a lot of money on these bargains. A lot of grocery store have meat they have marked down first thing in the morning.

- When an item you use regularly is on sale consider stocking up and buy as much as you can afford.

- If a sale item is out of stock ask for a raincheck if they offer them.

- Avoid the snack size bags of chips and cookies. It's better to buy the full-size bag and divide it up yourself.

- Check out discount store in your area. Dollar stores, Family Dollar, and discount grocery store can often save you more money.

- Keep a supply of basic staple foods. Flour, cornmeal, sugar, vegetable oil or lard, vegetables, milk, bread, eggs, cheese, or anything your family uses on a regular basis.

- Try not to waste food. Wasted food is wasted money.

- Don't buy foods that you or your family won't eat. Just because an item is on sale won't be money saved if you or your family won't eat it.

- Rotate pantry items, newer bought items in the back, older items in the front.

- Keep a check on foods expiration dates.

- Buy greeting cards, gift bags, gift wrap, party supplies, etc. at Dollar stores.

- Buy quality items that will last.

- Consider Jr. College or Tec to take core classes. Most credits will transfer to a University.

- Start a 504 College plan for children.

- Try to buy College text books used.

- Contact your professor if your struggling in class. They may tutor to prevent failure of a class and the extra expensive of retaking a course.

- If you are in need of specific items, let friends and family know before you buy.

Someone might have the item you are looking for and will either give it to you or sell it to you for cheap.

- Run appliances at off-peak times. Check with your power company to see when these times are.

- Cut up old clothing to use as rags. What better way to recycle.

- Keep some emergency cash handy. You never know when you might need it. It's better to plan ahead.

- Plant a garden for fresh vegetables. Compost food scraps to save on expensive soil additives.

- Be sure if an item has a rebate to fill out the form and submit it.

- Use money saving apps. Using these types of apps earns some of the cash back that you have already spent.

- Don't waste money on lotto tickets. The chances of winning are very slim.

- Save all your change. At the end of the year add it up and either save it or pay down a bill.

- Find cheap date ideas. Pop some popcorn and turn on a movie.

- Turn off the lights when you leave the room. There's no reason to have them on if you're not in there using them.

- Don't buy things you don't need. Skip buying the wants and focus only on what you truly need.

- Have a yard sale/garage sale to sell off items you no longer want. A great way to declutter and make a few extra dollars.

- Sell items online through sites like Ebay, Craigslist. You could even buy items wholesale to resell on these sites.

- Stop spending. Be happy with what you already have.

These tips have helped my family stretch our money, be able to save, and pay off debt. Not all of these tips will be practical to some people but I hope you find a few that you can use on your frugal living journey.